a farewell to everything

Also by Ilma Rakusa:

Poetry

Wie Winter
Les mots / morts
Ein Strich durch alles
Love after Love. Acht Abgesänge

Prose & Dramatic Works

Die Insel
Miramar
Steppe
Leben. Fünfzehn Akronyme
Sieben Dramolette

in English translation:

Steppe (translated by Solveig Emerson)

Essays

Farbband und Randfigur. Vorlesungen zur Poetik
Von Ketzern und Klassikern.
        Streifzüge durch die russische Literatur

Ilma Rakusa

A Farewell
to Everything

ninety nine-liners

translated by Andrew Shields & Andrew Winnard

Shearsman Books
Exeter

First published in the United Kingdom in 2005 by
Shearsman Books
58 Velwell Road
Exeter EX4 4LD

www.shearsman.com

ISBN 0-907562-77-9

Acknowledgements

We are grateful to Pro Helvetia, Arts Council of Switzerland, for their financial assistance in funding the translation of this volume, to Arts Council England for their support of Shearsman Books' 2005-2007 publishing programme.

Thanks are also due to Harald Ortlieb of Unternehmens.TV, GmbH, of Hamburg for permission to reproduce the photographs of the author on the cover, drawn from video recordings of the author reading at www.ilmarakusa.info.

ARTS COUNCIL ENGLAND

PRO HELVETIA
Arts Council of Switzerland

CONTENTS

In tercets to you

on seahorses airplanes

frigates on angels

cupids disguised

submarines

to you on November winds

at once to escape

the sport of waiting out

the countdown

(AW)

Don't play a Russian drama you

say and your voice scratches me raw

not unscathed I fall into your

heart the child in us lame

the mouth lost

then we scuffle home to

our seas

I'll give you yours and you

me mine with esteem

(AS)

I'm digging you out you say

I'm opening you up and making you happy

you say your laugh is the

lightest ever I'll never

do you harm you say

with pride and hold me for nights

on end in your arms

but when you leave

your promise is gone.

(AW)

Every time the leech

of the telephone sucks away my strength

these conversations mid-air idiosyncrasies

excitement at inopportune times when there's a need

for silence or the face to go with the voice

the complete person his

weight and time to bring

the mourning slowly

under control

(AW)

Cypresses on the skin
and (odour of cemetery) into your
arms the six thousand miles
westwards hugging the cushion
instead of me
a summer Sunday long or
hours that stab because my
light cannot reach
your night

(AW)

for Joseph Brodsky

Was the sofa red?
The case, actually the transatlantic trunk
stood there like a boat
bound for America.
Flag trunk books all
on an even keel. You left
so suddenly but from a need
and as it turned out
for ever. Now you are dead.

(AW)

for Joseph Brodsky

It snowed in Leningrad.
Night and the gas station
barren as fallow land. Streets
deserted façades void of
splendour. You went from there
on soft lips into the poem.
So it was that we drove quietly
and weightlessly through
your city. Not speaking.

(AW)

for Joseph Brodsky

The shoes the step
the street your face
in the middle. You stand
at the canalside in the light as if alarmed
and I don't know
what to say. Collar turned up
the word a fog in front of your mouth
rounded. So farewell.
For how many days?

(AW)

The quadrangle of childhood
with lighthouse and bay
with castle and box-
tree with veranda and fox
fables with strand and
Istrian sand with father
mother and breakers
with ice lolly and wind
from the karst but no fear

(AS)

Talking of sleep

of lying awake at night

when the fox barks

when the ambulance howls

when the sweat turns cold

when the child in the next room

rehearses his solitude

and the telephone suddenly flashes

why so green?

(AW)

When snow covers

the heath from what

distance do I say:

outland at home

you say: be

my wife

between hedgerow and sea

two tongues and

cold cold potpourri

(AS)

My parents the carpet
and me
the silence the foot
injury
no hurry the picture
immobility
good night the sheet
and a farewell
to everything

(AW)

Nine lines the length
of a note a gust of wind half a
thought an image in the basement of
incipient fears and a quick prayer
everything
and the desire for the whole thing
word hand warmth tango
land landscape and home
and sea sorely missed.

(AW)

The ferns slip into the river
mud flowing through Bohemia
the mosquito bites confuse
the long-tongued dogs
panting through the grass
a hiker is lying down
and the paper mill's
chimney stacks
breathe out their ragged gas

(AW)

The bridge stands back

the trains thunder on the track

the ticks lurk in the black

the river clots into slack

the sky is piercing

the man catching

sight of the woman pushing

his tongue into

her face

(AW)

Long tongues long miracles
when the peach eats its way into porcelain
and the milk laps at its dish
and the night crawls over the land
as softly as a toad and everything floats
I see your bright teeth over Alaska
your hands in the fish gut the rod
at your knee and our arctic hare
as a messenger lightning white

(AW)

From a glaciated migraine
Bashkir leaves thrust
where are the sheep the horns
the arm in the dust
holding sway
for everything turns and turns
and turns in a hilly rhythm
even the head burns
I cannot hold it anymore

(AS)

The branches have been

impounded the borders

are ablaze and such a

snow-white thing makes its

rounds below me

the grass is wounded

but the paws with pricked-up ears

and worse for wear still want to go

away

(AS)

Abigail and I don't know what

or why Abigail the wind

with its bull neck and

hurricane speed

it hums and thrums

and hisses biblical orchestrion

I say bellows casemate-black

ear strain and gales

so Abigail's addled

(AS)

Snow and the torch

as quiet as rice

the grains fall lightly

the yard disguised

the windows sprout

crystals and even

the freight with the stray

animal grows and throngs

overnight

(AS)

My dress shuts up on three floors

you devour time and steer the scorn

I read Exodus the Mount of Wind leaves us cold

the wandering sheets stare like basalt

in the catatonic house the mouth liberates

the tongue and the table wood abrades

voodoo reigns or lunacy here

where we were once one: ear

country throat

(AS)

I do not believe the curtain

blossoms so strangely before cypresses

it dresses the wind

hawks the interests

behind it sleep sleeps

and billows its tents

the world dwindles

in installments — I press

wallpaper apples

(AS)

If the oak is an ash it returns
home turns the slim
wand — sound wand — in wind
and shadow falls into the bath
the ornamental forms swim
on the grass tin zinc
subsides and in the boughs
the fifths flow both brass
and bamboo druidically

(AS)

for Friederike Mayröcker

The fur hat over the
eyelid and an age like dust
whiter than almost just
the hair rings bare
bast hair shaman straw
elation of another
kind in hoods you sing
the dream calls you by name
hoarse but HOLY AS

(AS)

Wedding breath (yes breath not wreath)
plus veil shade and now the white
of glaciers that displaces me
to childhood days replaces consummated
ceremonies shines to itself
a chamber play in how many parts
with woman man swaddled baby little
coach and four and not much sorrow
imprecisely pastoral no kneeling

(AS)

Flirting
with her mirror image
new bangs her face
so dressed up
almost lascivious
flashes no plastic glance
the woman sits in her eye
the word in her mouth
the melancholy in her collar

(AS)

That nothing (or nothing to say)

is not a carousel

no Pont Mirabeau

no stars over the Seine but rain

migraine and this horrific

film: three children's coffins small

smaller and he is alone

she alone not a pair

nightmare for all time

(AW)

Suspicion of writing like

scream me awake like

1. night wind

2. David and Gauloise

3. no time to lose

4. who was I thirty years ago

5. the Spring divides

6. keep on going

7. on pianos of words

(AW)

for Joseph Brodsky

For this death there is no rhyme
like an ice floe it drifts away
but where? The cold stands we are alone
and no escape succeeds
you loved moraines the Doric hair
of columns old plaster the coast of wavy
seas and what language washed up
on the shore of your tongue
shattered sound

(AS)

And the hard box tree in the park

between the busts of the musician

and the pilot

and the oval puddle reflecting

three Moorish arcades

black on the shore of the lost

and a half moon over Maria Formosa

and the odor of childhood

when the swing blows

(AS)

With two tongues

child's tongue for treats

and cooking croquettes

for stains cookies

and indoor disasters

the other tongue writes

to ward off the scream

the fences stand between

the oceans and are silent

(AW)

To the hairdresser with
a light step on dry ground
back through the snow
like a very old lady
from fence to fence
down the slope and nobody
no footprints only night
only a car
follows my fear

(AS)

Father reads the paper

Mother reads

and I am at home

under Chagall's palette

with an injured foot

that ran for a bet

whether the child lying down

would arise

instead of the hag

(AW)

Meadow

this word like

no likeness only a breath

of wind from the Maira and

a little birch wood

the sky steals

into the night

the beetle into

the bark

(AS)

In the quick March snow through the city

blows a cool omen

trousers wide a hope that doesn't speak

my hat is lost

a friend mourns the dog

ducks in the frost

the lake is a pond

I search for your face

fed up with this loneliness

(AW)

Brown hair powerful lines
the oval poem (from Rome
spring sends greetings) vows
no fight no lyre
no verdict but you
your face bright with the new
and a mosaic frieze of light
on lashes cheek brow
rhymed stroke for stroke

(AS)

Disreputable steps or
strawberry-red high up
into brighter zones
to where talk dances
over tea and bread and
light from the roof domains
the heart has tact the
love untracked what do the crows
in the park have to say

(AS)

They are romping in the moor pond

three boys with a dog one

with a red cap

but a belt of blue

the others brown and

arms held high

and bubbles in the water

sunbeaten joy like

the uphill paths heading back

(AW)

In the train just dozing off
when the horizon tips inward
this sandhill yellow and huge
African it towers up
behind the tracks of a
provincial station vastly different
Where am I? and deep red a
bulldozer enters the picture
to take down the illusion

(AS)

Does life only take place outside
the venetian blinds? Who says
the silent box with the stone tiles
is dead? Who? Here light-rabbits run
and epiphanies rage the apple falls
without a sound from the tree and the crickets
trill in my ears it is not a question
of willing where I am namely
before the wall in the paper

(AS)

The scenery without you
and as I turn around
to the couples alone

even crying's no help
time has sprouted hair
the agony has teeth

and you so far away
between killer whales
caught by the rift

(AW)

Exhausted three times over
twice deadheaded by the pain
and the hands tremble again

rage has no manners to keep
it screams out loud in the night
frightening the animals

belief is frozen
the day's work festers
it's called love

(AW)

Tracks snow

emptily the night comes on

who am I

or you with your power

to separate us

drink coffee

the sky laughs

dolphins palms

all in spite

(AW)

No further is cruel

like a fence

and the hours pass

in a circle spoiling

the straw the boat

and so on

I clear my heart

lace up my dress

consult the horoscope

(AW)

The evening protects
only the black
is darker than the cafard
the afflicted memory
than your parting word
rammed into my breast
than the coarse kernels
of corrosion than the scorn
of this operation to death

(AS)

The glance at the hand that creases

a slatted hand many stories

and the arm stiff with pain

an old arm may not lift

any weights even the ivory keys hurt

the handshake farewell to piano

to greeting the trembling pencil errs

across the paper seeks lines sense

reason

(AS)

Coincidences or what
in the photo the child deep in grass
a rear view and the fox searches
searches for the vixen
barking deep into the night
so much wind prowls around the house
and two o'clock what is that clattering
a curtain in the picture hard or
green no doors

(AW)

In the cinema in my head

the lake flickers red

wrinkles the skin

I want to come in he commands

get out swells

the dream has a cord

loose

and no man leads me

out of the lake

(AW)

Nothing against the Egyptian couple

staring into the distance

for millennia stony and silent

him to the right her to the left in unquestioning

juxtaposition only I do not know

what use it is to you and me to sit here

with feverish knees and furtive

glances into the pockets of

fate: where are we?

(AW)

The plum-tree blossom
is almost Japanese the white
light on the slope that trembles
creases under ragged clouds
the day greets us greyly throws
open garish windows for
birds fools woeful hearts
and scatters a laconic sprinkle
of snow

(AW)

In the post office to while away the time

the flickering disaster stories

news in brief and casual

apodictics no one looks over

or dumb like Behemoth

only the children the illiterate

show feelings and the camellia

behind the counter is redder

than anything in this crowd

(AW)

The neighbour sneezes

an allergic length of time

almost a cry for help

each time a semi-tone

higher and there is no one

warding off his complaints

the friend dead

the man alone

beaten

(AW)

I stumble through the day
from sleep to sleep
the autumnal swoon
I say the early snow
the changing years the riot
of words noise routine and
deadlines the pale grey the
piles of newspapers no bees
stealing nectar

(AW)

Does the asphalt know

what happens next

or should I ask

the fortune-teller? Thinking

of fate's magic

I must laugh in the night

like a child and in my half-sleep state

blinder than Marina

Tsvetaeva

(AW)

When you call from the beach
from the three-quarter restaurant
with the tops of the palm trees
while standing or perhaps
parcelled out between customers
and suspicions of rapid greed —
I grip your voice
in my hand pay heed
scribble you on the paper

(AS)

Paradisical the House of
the White Dove beside the
House of the Wolf the animals
(insignia) united the
hotels flourish and no one
laments innocence
it has pinions a
tail domestic manners
and talons of metal

(AS)

Whether moon whether white

the bastion or blue

at day's edge or place

three domes or

twilight sentence there

lie the dead there

the fortress frees the

sky the moment is right

sets

(AS)

Inside the pub the warmth

the pale wine the table-wood

full of names the farm-oven

the chirruping voices

no ladies the paper with the Irishman's

features the Cyrillic scrawl

on all fours and we

two gypsies for a time

far from it all united sublime

(AW)

The road is straight as
the rod solid but
not a shelter and ever onward
how I wish for a torrent
something roaring and
on the horizon a touch
of uproar just so or
so no routine sets in
in the daily labour of loving

(AS)

The silence hangs

the horse and the hand

the head and the wall

the seat the steam the train

the clock the book

the handkerchief and the pain

all ready for goodbye

only it's you who's going

away

(AW)

Into your arms

(odour of cypress tree)

which six thousand miles

west from here caress

the pillow instead of me

a summer sunday long

and time that's wrong

because my sun my light

cannot reach your night

The racket subsided
dead factories the soundtrack
of night and a neon sign
ZÜRICH LIFE insures
power but here inside
the pair of cats with Tokay
canvas paintbrush calm or
maybe not the ice doll thaws
the girlfriend laughs

(AS)

The nut tree at eight o'clock

sunlit like Cape Sounion

only better roots

a happier trunk

its bark more lined

full of beetles and wind

stands aslant lives its

time and passes — which

the pillars can but dream of

(AS)

Quaking grass two deer lethargy
dramatic cloud formation clover my knee
scuttled and dust chestnut leaves

summer never hung lower a parody
of itself crickets the shoe how does it weep
nature and how do the beasts

demoiselles immortelles pale harmony
the roosters sleep the sky see
in agony

(AS)

The fountain is fit to be tied

the book of margins is wide

awake as a waiting room

both so wild and at night

not two but many

voices signify

a half euphoria

or a whole fight

so Europe such a sigh

(AS)

Fish or phantom

and red the cloud

now carmine

will suffice

I will not cower

anymore you've got your time

your sea even the void

is good

between fighters

(AS)

You want me flat as a plane
and misjudge the mania
of such correction urbane

as you are: you refrain
from explanation on the train
of success the cellophane

world replaces the hurricane
the sorrow my bane
do you sense it now? End

(AS)

Sleeping and
bathing like
a child has a
spoon and digs
itself free
the moon hangs in the forest
its light sloping in
on to the soap
in my lap

(AW)

The bread is burnt

the pencil trembles in my hand

my tongue is cramped

eyes crying no tears

a leaden heart

head splitting apart

the cupboards are bare

silent the house where

he doesn't come any more

(AW)

In the honeycombs of the floors
he wanders around terracotta gaze
no exit

meanders inward leans
on Indian palankeens silk
twill

gets tangled in woods where
the branches stare and fate says
nothing

(AS)

Count the alarm bells
in C-sharp in D-sharp the highest
notes of doubt of friction
of incongruence
lie down to be healed
in the familiar bed
alone like a finger
and tussle with the
soul's ruckus

(AS)

for Gennady Aygi

Where Chuvashia is where

Samara on which Volga bend

where the steppe the horse

where the motherland

where the rectangle of the grave

where the sand where the children's

songs where poplars time

where the toy soldiers

is I

(AS)

for Gennady Aygi

We could be more like the Huns
you and I we could ride
argue o grass o shout o soil
the hills with bright hooves
in the hour between hound
and wolf and so on
but riding through the writing pad
needs no whip the scab of
letters no wound o barbarian sin

(AW)

The lake is a plate today

a mirror and in the Russian

woman's book a girdle of birds

the first lover is named Pushkin

the second brother

the third just another

the fourth just lover

separate ribs territories

and a woman skipping

(AS)

for Valeria Narbikova

Bonds of merry madness

small bones from the Crimea around my wrist

a yellow dog collar in my pocket

(a find from Vienna)

candles on the Irishman's grave

apple vodka bottle

running up and down on the lake's bank

feeding birds etc.

then the extravagant escape on the wing

(AW)

This billygoat dozes
a sleep so white
with lightly posed
limbs his beard nods
slightly his horn is stiff
his hooves turn in
and his face grins
with lids shut tight
with a nirvana look

(AS)

A table with toy animals

rice tabasco and a curious tin

put money in and it springs

open a hand grasps poisonous green

for the metal and snap

the lacquered black

coffin snaps shut the host laughs

the joke is fun the tea

frozen in our glasses

(AW)

I cannot help my
Magdalena this
prodigy of whys
woes wondering
up to her eyes
in the word
comfort none
or in death
through the letters

(AS)

The goodbye cuts
a knee in the gut
needles piercing my calves
a heart like lead that
no longer wants to beat
my saliva dries up at
the word my head
is empty and silence
has the say

(AW)

Jim she says it wears me down and out.

Ann he says I am not a lout.

It goes and goes on and is a stalemate

or (to be honest) checkmate.

Two love each other want the best

but the best for whom. The days

pass the uniting bed becomes

an abacus. Only sadness and anger remain

spontaneous. Who will bow out?

(AS)

We danced

four matrons a full house

we stamped Russian

laughed Prussian

made like gypsies

we were old and were young

we spoke Babylonian higgledy-piggledy

of loves and risks

and monogamously went to sleep

(AS)

How swiftly the Atlantic
puts itself between us
when my own sun goes down
you are standing in SoHo's light chewing
a bagel and look pleased but differently so
your laugh still fills my
mouth but the Hungarian leads me
roughly and expertly to Buchenwald
so there I am – and you?

(AW)

Not a princess —

a night owl a dormouse

a childwoman a sea dreamer

a fast walker a piano player

a bookworm an anchoress

a note collector a cicada girl

a world explorer a mind tripper

a desert fox a scaredy cat

a daddy's girl and your pleasure

(AS)

The accusation is a slap in the face
into the plate the voice cleaves
shriller than steel it leaves
no choice the throat turns cold
the ice and the candle weeps old
no one knows why there's a duel
the oath skinless we stand there cruelly
wounded knocked off course
not a couple

(AW)

Under the picture the sleep of
the cherry-red Japanese woman I mean
mouth that simply waits
until evening falls and the
margins of therapy break down
am I a head as racked as
it is black or submarine but
what's the name of the girl
from Fukui with the braid?

(AS)

To rearrange my mind
move sleep from right to left
the books and teddy bears
the spoons and hinges
to redream the nightmares
and be white
and be light
I mean threadbare dreamless
with a view of the cataract

(AS)

The summer should be a canopy

a panoramic house

and I, in the middle, with no

departure-times deadlines lists

the birchtree is standing still the day wafts

indoors has its sound

the shadows fit together

soon even the words themselves

do so without congestion

(AW)

In the breaks between the trees: snow
in the spaces between the words: snow
in the hollows between the houses: snow
in the yards between the fences: snow
and cold
in the ponds between the pubs: snow
in the holes between the oaks: snow
in the dreams between the fields: snow
in the plates and pleats: snow

(AS)

I ran through the night
into the old vacated house
with the wooden staircase
the floor creaks the crew is
awake exhibition makers
Père et fils a white covered
table invites me we dine
in frugal finery minus cutlery
tomatoes cheese Easter hare

(AW)

The vice of desolation

the courtyard of isolation

the water of futility

we loudly criticise

Peace! shouts all of America

we vigorously applaud

the world a ball the house

a lair of ugly feelings

and war on all chairs

(AW)

Places and Dates of Composition of the Original Texts

Page 9: Zürich, 6.11.96; 10: Zürich, 8.3.96; p.11: Zürich, 15.1.96; p.12: Zürich, 21.7.96; p.13: Zürich, 21.7.96; p.14: New York, 4.12.96; p.15: New York, 4.12.96; p.16: Zürich, 11.12.96; p.17: Munich, 22.11.96; p.18: Zürich, 29.9.96; p.19: Munich, 22.11.96; p.20: Zürich, 9.3.96; p.21: Zürich, 21.7.96; p.22: Havlíčkův Brod, 19.7.95; p.23: Havlíčkův Brod, 19.7.95; p.24: Venasque, 2.8.95; p.25: Zürich, 4.6.95; p.26: Zürich, 4.6.95; p.27: Zürich, 5.6.95; p.29: Venasque, 6.8.95; p.30: Saint Rémy, 15.6.95; p.31: Stuttgart (Schloß Solitude), 17.7.96; p.32: Zürich, 17.11.95; p.33: Zürich, 10.3.97; p.34: Zürich, 3.10.96; p.35: Zürich, 9.3.97; p.36: Zürich, 26.2.97; p.37: Zürich, 31.1.96; p.38: Venice, 4.1.96; p.39: Zürich, 6.11.96; p.40: Zürich, 27.11.96; p.41: Zürich, 9.3.96; p.42: Bondo, 4.8.96; p.43: Zürich, 15.2.97; p.44: Zürich, 1.2.97; p.45: Zürich, 18.2.97; p.46: Zürich, 6.10.96; p.47: Zürich, 4.10.96; p.48: Zürich, 2.8.96; p.49: Bondo, 6.8.96; p.50: Zürich, 20.2.97; p.51: Zürich, 19.1.97; p.52: Bondo, 5.8.96; p.53: Zürich, 19.1.97; p.54: Zürich, 15.2.97; p.55: Zürich, 13.2.97; p.56: Zürich, 1.10.96; p.57: Zürich, 23.1.96; p.58: Zürich, 29.3.97; p.59: Zürich, 24.2.97; p.60: Zürich, 16.8.96; p.61: Zürich, 6.10.96; p.62: Bondo, 5.8.96; p.63: Zürich, 1.10.96; p.64: Salzburg, 20.12.96; p.65: Salzburg, 20.12.96; p.66: Zürich, 30.11.96; p.67: Zürich, 28.9.96; p.68: Zürich, 31.3.96; p.69: Zürich, 30.11.96; p.70: Zürich, 21.2.97; p.71: Bondo, 24.8.96; p.72: Bondo, 8.8.96; p.73: Bondo, 8.8.96; p.74: Bondo, 4.8.96; p.75: Bondo, 5.8.96; p.76: Zürich, 20.2.97; p.77: Zürich, 13.1.97; p.78: Zürich, 1.2.97; p.79: Zürich, 18.1.96; p.80: Zürich, 19.3.97; p.81: Zürich, 19.3.97; p.82: Zürich, 20.2.97; p.83: Zürich, 30.11.96; p.84: Zürich, 6.10.96; p.85: Zürich, 6.10.96; p.86: Zürich, 1.12.96; p.87: Zürich, 15.1.96; p.88: Zürich, 14.2.97; p.89: Zürich, 27.11.96; p.90: Zürich, 8.3.96; p.91: Zürich, 14.2.97; p.92: Zürich, 15.1.97; p.93: Zürich, 20.7.96; p.94: Zürich, 4.6.95; p.95: Zürich, 20.3.97; p.96; Zürich, 18.3.97; p.97: Zürich, 20.3.97; p.98: Zürich, 10.3.97.

Note:
Poem 61 (page 69 'Into your arms. . .') was written in English.

The Translators

Andrew Shields has a Ph.D. in Comparative Literature from the University of Pennsylvania, and has been teaching at the University of Basel since 1995. His poems, prose, and translations have appeared in journals and books on both sides of the Atlantic. His first collection of poems, *Your Mileage May Vary,* is looking for a publisher. Recently published volumes include poems by Dieter M Gräf, a novel by Michael Krüger, and the *Letters* of Hannah Arendt and Martin Heidegger.

Andrew Winnard is an accomplished translator of German, whose work includes two published translations of full-length books. One of these was short-listed for the Schlegel-Tieck Translation Prize. He has also translated many articles for peer-reviewed journals, for *The Guardian*, and numerous commercial organisations and agencies. As a graduate student he won the Felicia Heman poetry prize. More recently he has been Translations Manager for the publisher Polity Press, and since 1998 has been Cambridge University Press's chief editor for languages and linguistics.